D1520600

UNDERSTANDING ADHD

JESSICA RUSICK

Big Buddy Books

An Imprint of Abdo Publishing
abdobooks.com

abdobooks.com

Published by Abdo Publishing, a division of ABDO, PO Box 398166, Minneapolis, Minnesota 55439.
Copyright © 2022 by Abdo Consulting Group, Inc. International copyrights reserved in all countries.
No part of this book may be reproduced in any form without written permission from the publisher.
Big Buddy Books™ is a trademark and logo of Abdo Publishing.

Printed in the United States of America, North Mankato, Minnesota.
052021
092021

THIS BOOK CONTAINS
RECYCLED MATERIALS

Design: Emily O'Malley, Mighty Media, Inc.
Production: Mighty Media, Inc.
Editor: Megan Borgert-Spaniol
Content Consultant: Brenda Blackmore, Special Education Director
Cover Photographs: Shutterstock Images
Interior Photographs: Shutterstock Images

Library of Congress Control Number: 2020949918

Publisher's Cataloging-in-Publication Data
Names: Rusick, Jessica, author.
Title: Understanding ADHD / by Jessica Rusick
Description: Minneapolis, Minnesota : Abdo Publishing, 2022 | Series: Understanding disabilities | Includes
    online resources and index.
Identifiers: ISBN 9781532195716 (lib. bdg.) | ISBN 9781098216443 (ebook)
Subjects: LCSH: Attention-deficit hyperactivity disorder--Juvenile literature. | Attention-deficit-disordered
    youth--Juvenile literature. | Attention-deficit hyperactivity disorder--Diagnosis--Juvenile literature. |
    Social acceptance--Juvenile literature.
Classification: DDC 618.928589--dc23

CONTENTS

Test Day

It's test day in Julian's class. During the test, Julian has trouble **focusing**. He hears a classmate drop a pencil. He sees a bird fly by the window. Soon after, he hears footsteps in the hall.

Julian's classmates seem to tune out these sights and sounds. But Julian finds them **distracting**. When he is distracted, he feels like a million thoughts are bouncing around in his head. That's because Julian has ADHD.

What Is ADHD?

ADHD stands for attention-deficit/hyperactivity disorder. This condition can make it hard for people to pay attention and control their **behavior**. All kids have trouble **focusing** or behaving at times. But for kids with ADHD, these are daily **challenges**.

ADHD is a **developmental** disability. It can affect how a person moves, speaks, learns, or behaves. Someone with ADHD may behave differently than you. But it's important to accept and **appreciate** people's differences.

Breaks to move around or play can help kids with ADHD focus better in class.

7

You can show you accept and **appreciate** others by trying to learn more. You might politely ask if they'll share with you how ADHD affects them. And always use respectful language. Name-calling is never okay.

Remember

People with disabilities are not **victims**. This word makes it sound like having a disability is a bad thing. But a disability is not bad. It's just a difference!

Listen and give support to friends when they share their feelings.

9

ADHD Symptoms

There are three types of ADHD. Doctors have found common **behaviors** for each type. However, not everyone who displays these behaviors has ADHD.

ADHD affects everyone differently. Some people take **medicine** for their **symptoms**. Some may also work on their behaviors with **therapists**.

Inattentive Type

Some people with ADHD have mostly inattentive **behaviors**. These include:

- ★ Trouble **focusing**
- ★ Hard time staying **organized**
- ★ Getting bored easily
- ★ Hard time listening to or following directions
- ★ Losing or forgetting things often
- ★ Trouble feeling interested in or excited to do something

Hyperactive-Impulsive Type

Others with ADHD have mostly hyperactive and impulsive **behaviors**. These include:

* ★ Doing or saying things without thinking
* ★ Talking a lot
* ★ Interrupting others
* ★ Trouble sitting still
* ★ Hard time finishing a task before starting another
* ★ Getting upset easily and having trouble calming down

Combined Type

Most people with ADHD have a mix of inattentive, hyperactive, and impulsive behaviors.

A doctor asks questions to find out if a kid has ADHD. These questions are often about challenges at school.

Who Has ADHD?

Kids with ADHD usually begin showing **symptoms** between ages three and six. The symptoms of ADHD can lessen with age. But they often continue into adulthood.

ADHD is common. In the United States, more than 6 million kids have it! Doctors are more likely to recognize ADHD in males than in females. Doctors believe this is because females with ADHD often have less noticeable symptoms.

ADHD Symptoms in Males and Females

Males with ADHD tend to show more noticeable **symptoms** than females with ADHD.

Males

★ Acting suddenly without thinking

★ Very active

★ Trouble paying attention

★ Forceful with body

Females

★ Shy or not social

★ Nervous or fearful

★ Trouble paying attention

★ Forceful with words

ADHD at School

School can be hard for kids with ADHD. In classrooms, students must follow rules like sitting still and paying attention. Kids with ADHD can find this **challenging**. So, they may get in trouble for **misbehaving**.

Kids with ADHD often feel misunderstood when they get in trouble. This is because they are not misbehaving on purpose. It's just harder for them to control their behaviors.

Kids with ADHD may take tests in a room with fewer **distractions**. They may also play with small toys during class. This helps kids quietly let out **energy** while still paying attention to schoolwork.

Students with ADHD can work with their teachers to limit classroom distractions.

Squeeze balls help kids with ADHD to relax and focus when they are feeling restless.

Fidget cubes have buttons, switches, and other parts that keep a user's fingers busy. This helps the user let out nervous or bored energy.

A kneaded eraser can be balled up, squeezed, and stretched. This helps a user's mind stay focused while his or her hands stay busy.

Making Friends

Everyone needs friendship. But kids with ADHD can have trouble making friends. This can be due to their **behavior**. For example, they may forget to share toys. Or, they may get **distracted** while someone is talking to them. These behaviors can upset other kids. So, kids with ADHD may be left out or teased by their peers. Being left out makes people feel bad about themselves.

A kid with ADHD may want to be part of a group activity but feel unsure of how to join in.

Being a Friend

Everyone has his or her own strengths and **challenges**. That's okay! No matter what, everyone should be treated with respect.

There are many ways to be a good friend to someone with ADHD. Tell him when he does something well. Offer to help her study for tests. And, tell an adult if your friend is being teased.

Be **patient** and forgiving. A friend with ADHD may act in ways that make you feel mad or sad. Always speak up if your feelings are hurt. But remember that your friend likely didn't mean to upset you.

A study partner can help a student with ADHD keep track of homework.

More Ways to Be a Friend

Be Kind and Curious

Ask if your friend wants to share what it's like to have ADHD. If he does, listen and ask respectful questions.

Come Up with a Secret Sign

For example, tap your nose if you notice your friend interrupting someone. This will remind her to let others finish their thoughts.

Give Space

Give your friend time and space to work through her feelings.

Strengths

Having ADHD can be **challenging**. However, many people say it helps them to be creative and **energetic**. People with ADHD have become successful sports stars, **astronauts**, and more.

Simone Biles

Simone Biles is a **gymnast** with ADHD. She is known as one of the greatest gymnasts of all time! Biles has won four Olympic gold medals and 25 world **championship** medals. She has said that her ADHD is "nothing to be ashamed of."

Simone Biles at the 2016 Olympics in Brazil

Golden Rules

Millions of people have disabilities. If you know someone with a disability, there may be times when you feel unsure of what to say or do. When in doubt, remember to treat others how you'd want to be treated. And, keep in mind these other golden rules:

★ Accept and respect differences

★ Use respectful language

★ Be kind and caring

Activities

Do you have any friends who have ADHD? Invite them to join you for a fun activity.

Have a dance party

Build a fort

Go for a bike ride

GLOSSARY

appreciate—to value or admire greatly.

astronaut—a person who is trained for space travel.

behave—to act in a certain way. Behavior is the way a person acts. To misbehave is to behave badly.

challenge (CHA-luhnj)—something that tests one's strengths or abilities.

championship—a game, a match, or a race held to find a first-place winner.

developmental—relating to the steps of natural growth.

distract—to cause to turn away from one's original focus. A distraction is something that causes one to be distracted.

energy—the ability to move, work, or play hard without getting tired. To be energetic is to be active and full of energy.

focus (FOH-kuhs)—to give full attention to a task.

gymnast—a person who practices gymnastics, a sport of strength, balance, and other skills.

medicine (MEH-duh-suhn)—an item used in or on the body to treat an illness, ease pain, or heal a wound.

organized—skilled at arranging or planning things.

patient—calm and kind when waiting for something or dealing with challenges.

symptom—a noticeable change in the normal working of the body or mind.

therapist—a person who helps people deal with challenging events or feelings by talking about them.

victim—someone who has been harmed by an unpleasant event.

ONLINE RESOURCES

Booklinks
NONFICTION NETWORK
FREE! ONLINE NONFICTION RESOURCES

To learn more about ADHD, please visit **abdobooklinks.com** or scan this QR code. These links are routinely monitored and updated to provide the most current information available.